OPPORTUNITY CO$T INVESTING

What You **MUST** Know About Opportunity Cost

Make More By Losing Less

JESSIE RANCOURT

Jessie M. Rancourt, MBA
What You Need to Know About Opportunity Cost

50% of the proceeds from this book are donated to charity

www.jessierancourt.com

This book is dedicated to my siblings,

Scott, Ali, and Kevin.

Contents

Figures

Tables

Introduction

Your largest cost, opportunity cost, is one you will never see. Yet, more discussion on opportunity cost is desperately needed in the financial world. The foremost reasons are our limited understanding of the true value of costs, inexperience with measuring true performance, and innate psychological tendencies that largely affect our execution. These factors undermine our focus to the opportunities that will provide the most benefit. In turn, these factors inhibit our ability to communicate costs and performances to others, escalating the cause for concern.

How many times have we heard discussions such as, "I made $100 in AAPL" or "I made 20% on my last trade"? These fragments of financial decisions, unbeknownst to the person saying it, are harmful. It does not give us the full picture and perpetuates poor behavior.

When we do not know how to accurately calculate and communicate opportunities, but do so, the inefficiently cascades. Fortunately, the converse is also true. The more we can do to get the value of our opportunity cost as true-to-life as possible, the better we can communicate opportunities with others. Inadvertently, others will be more likely to do the same, compounding into a positive effect.

To learn opportunity cost we must start at the basics. This book will walk you through what opportunity cost is, tools to value and communicate the true value of your costs and your performances, introduce the psychology of opportunity cost, and suggest ways to improve your search for opportunities.

Of course, knowing is only a fraction of the battle. So, on every step of the way you should act, not just read, to accomplish the full power of what I hope this book is meant for. Even if this means merely pointing you in the direction of a new opportunity.

Chapter 1: What Is Opportunity Cost

Opportunity cost is "The cost of something in terms of an opportunity forgone. Opportunity cost is given by the benefits that could have been obtained by choosing the best alternative opportunity [1]." In other words, opportunity cost is how much we *lost out on* by not choosing the best option for us. It sounds nonsensical and contrary to psychological egoism, choosing an option that is not the best for us, but it is a product of the psychological irrationalities that make us human. That is only the beginning because the concept of opportunity cost extends far beyond evaluating alternatives.

*The best possible gain of **ALL** opportunities*
*– The gain made on the **CHOSEN** opportunity*
Opportunity Cost

You will hardly ever see opportunity cost come up on measuring a person's net worth, a company's financial statements, or investor reports, but it has tremendous and real consequences. This is no surprise because saying that opportunity cost is hard to identify, never mind attribute a value to, would be an understatement. In fact, due to the complexity of its nature, we cannot quantify opportunity cost exactly, but we can come close enough where we can make rational decisions.

The salient reason for this is our propensity to vastly underestimate the real costs of an opportunity. Beyond the scope of your actual costs are related ancillary effects compounding positively or negatively. Also, there are variably valued items that not only make it hard to attach a value, but also impossible to translate from one person to the next. Albeit hard to calculate, the relative opportunity cost helps the decision making process that improves our finances.

Part 1:

Cost Factors

Chapter 2: Opportunity Cost Matrix

MEASURING COST FACTORS

Capital allocation and *time allocation* are the two factors that comprise the cost consideration in **mathematical opportunity cost.** *Capital allocation* is your ability to move money around to create value and *time allocation* is how efficiently you manage your time.

You unlock your greatest potential when you can master both *capital allocation* and *time allocation*. If a person is great at *capital allocation* but lacks *time allocation,* then although they have a well-established, efficient foundation, they will not have the cash flow to support modest-sized advances in wealth. This would be like someone who can return 20% on their money but has a dismal earnings power of minimum wage. Inversely, an individual who can manage their time, get paid hundreds of thousands of dollars as a salary, yet not know how to invest, will suffer from of a poor foundation.

For example, if you had a small, dollar capped security that yielded 1% and you found a new opportunity that yielded 1.01%, *capital allocation* would suggest this is a no-brainer transfer, but *time allocation* might suggest that the value of your time is wasted switching. Sometimes accepting a lower percentage return yields better results if the dollar reward comes in stronger.

We will expand on these two concepts by breaking the fourth wall and evaluating the opportunity cost of purchasing this book.

***

If a 25-year-old paid $20 for this book, what is the *value* that would need to be returned to have bested the almighty opportunity cost? Remember this example because we will use it throughout the book. The two largest factors of opportunity cost in this example are the cost of the book and the time spent engaged in the book. Add to this the best available use of the 8 hours it took to read the book, in our instance, working 8 hours overtime (1.5 times pay on a salary of $52,145.80, the national average [2]). In total, the $20 book became a *present value* cost of $320.84[i].

---

[i] Ignoring taxes and other miscellaneous items for simplicity. We will include the minutiae as the book progresses.

$$\$20\ Book\ Value + \left(\frac{\begin{matrix}\$52{,}145.80\\ Salary\end{matrix}}{\begin{matrix}2080\ Annual\\ Work\ Hours\end{matrix}} * 8\ Hours\ of\ Work * 1.5\ Overtime\ Multiple \right) = \$320.84$$

Present value (PV) is the worth of something in the current moment, which in our example, is when the book is purchased and read. To demonstrate the importance that our decisions have, we should also look at what our 25-year-old gave up by "judgment day" which, for simplicity, is retirement 40 years later at age 65. In the financial world, we call the amount later in time the *future value* (FV). This method has been demonstrated in the book, *The Compound Effect* by Darren Hardy, and is an excellent tool for your analysis because it shows the lasting effects our decisions make. If our 25-year-old has only ever known their bank account that makes 0.07% interest (the national average [3]) their $20 purchase cost, with the $300.84 that could have been earned with their time, equates to $329.95. Essentially, they are giving up $320.84 today, or $329.95 by retirement (nominally), to purchase and read this book. Therefore, this book needs to return to the reader that much or more value (no pressure).

$$Nominal\ FV = \$320.84 * (1 + 0.07\%)^{40} = \$329.95$$

On the surface $329.95 sounds like a large hurdle, but if our parable person learned how to save only $8.14 a year by reading this book, a profit would have been made. What financial or self-help book has not delivered that value? Even if one fails to do so, the average benefit of these books is significant enough to conclude that **these books pay you to read them!**

***

The culmination of measuring mathematical opportunity cost with the present and future costs of capital and time allocation results in the opportunity cost matrix. This graphic was created to alleviate some of the pain because evaluating *mathematical opportunity cost* can get dense and confusing.

	Capital Allocation	**Time Allocation**
Present Costs	Present Costs of Capital Allocation	Present Costs of Time Allocation
Future Costs	Future Costs of Capital Allocation	Future Costs of Time Allocation

Going forward we will separate measuring opportunity costs by capital allocation or time allocation and further separate those categories by present costs or future costs. There is no hard line between the categories, they are plainly a way to organize our thoughts and make sure we cover as many details of an opportunity cost equation that we can. Because underestimating the *real costs* is our single greatest weakness in evaluating the cost factors of our opportunity cost, it is important that we give ourselves as many chances to get all the details as we can.

The immeasurable, yet *real*, costs attributed to *mathematical opportunity cost* become particularly difficult due to how overwhelming plentiful, varying in value person to person, and incalculable the compounding effects can be. If you and your partner set a rule for going out to eat only once a week and break the rule "just this once," what are the odds it will happen again? Probably high. What are the odds there is a "catch-up" factor that leads us to be worse off than the consistent behavior prior? Again, likely high.

As an example of the opportunity cost matrix in work we can use the purchase of a video game console. How many people buy a video game console and a single game for $400 and neglect to factor in that they have immediately locked in costs for future video game purchases. After all it makes sense, why spend $400 to play one game? We likely do not know how many games we would purchase but statistically it will be more resulting in a commitment to more capital and time.

It almost seems silly of us to suggest these minutiae are a big deal but because *it is real,* we must factor for it. And because they almost seem silly to us, we vastly underestimate the *real costs* of a purchase leading to what I believe is the largest contributor to incorrect evaluations of the cost factor in opportunity cost. This results in an uncomfortable scenario where, although we do not know the value that *future costs* hold, we must because they do count. Often these *future costs* become a greater deal than any *present cost* will ever be. But because we tragically can never be exact, all you need to aim for is as close as possible and set a margin of error.

Chapter 3: The Intrinsic Way

A note before we progress, a fundamental flaw exists in calculating opportunity cost in the example we worked out, which is relating the opportunity cost of reading a book to the average American, which I did for relatability. Intrinsically, the best way to definitively prove the value is to account for individuals in the highest echelon of *capital allocation* and *time allocation*. After all, if we can prove the value for even the greatest earners, would that not prove it for everyone else? This mental model, popularized by the late philosopher Karl Popper, is called falsification, and represents trying to disprove your opportunity as the best one. If it fails the test, a double negative, it is the proven superior. Essentially, we want to stack the odds against the value we are trying to create and see if it can still pull out ahead. Conversely, if the opportunity is shown to be inferior, you must trade positions and try it again. Consequently, if both pass against each other more analysis is required. This could potentially mean the analysis requires more details, a different method, a risk analysis, or the opportunities are equal enough where the difference is insignificant.

Chapter 4: Present Costs of Capital Allocation

When we think of measuring opportunity cost the capital allocation, or financial aspect, is what comes first to our mind. The *present costs of capital allocation* are therefore the sum of the dollars currently lost out on by choosing one alternative over another. To study *present costs of capital allocation* we must break it down into the cashflows and the balances.

CASHFLOW AND ADDED COSTS

A book might cost us $20 but did we buy coffee while we were shopping? Ancillary costs that were made with direct causation to the primary purchase should be added to the cost of the primary purchase. Whether we want to recognize it or not, these additional items are real, and they really matter. Below is an example breakdown of measuring the cost of buying a book at a bookstore:

$$
\begin{array}{lr}
 & \$20\ \textit{Book purchase} \\
 & \$2.50\ (\textit{Buying a } \$5.00\ \textit{coffee about half the time}) \\
 & \$0.575/\textit{mile}\ (\textit{wear, tear, depreciation, and gas of car}) \\
 & \textit{Increase on insurance for increased mileage} \\
 & \textit{Cost of increased risk of car accident} \\
+ & \textit{All Cashflow and Added Costs} \\
\hline
 & \boldsymbol{\textit{Total Present Cost of Capital Allocation}}
\end{array}
$$

Again, opportunity cost might come off as nit-picking, but these factors are real. Eventually, you will find that the minutiae become insignificant and probabilities can be indeterminable, but it can be solved by logically rounding. As you will see, opportunity cost is not a measurable item and we are only aiming for as close as possible. However, without studying the *present costs of capital allocation* we might miss important factors. It could be very likely that instead of the $2.50 coffee factor it could have been eating out for lunch entirely and a dramatic increase of the overall cost. Even an alternative, online shopping, has its considerations. How many times have we added items from our cart so we can reach a free shipping minimum? How about adding discretionary items into the cart, moving saved items into the cart, or succumbing to an advertisement or discount?

Opportunities can be applied the same way as with purchases. If you are deciding which company to invest your IRA with you will need to gather every present cost that you can reasonably manage. Despite taxes, fees, and expense rations often being the largest contributors, push yourself to look beyond them and find more present costs of capital allocation that might be specific to you.

BALANCES AND INDIVIDUAL RATE OF RETURN

You probably noticed that the *present value* cost of the book for the average American was $320.84 while the *future value* was only slightly more, $329.95. We attributed this to the measly 0.07% bank account APY and our parable person's *individual rate of return*. To illustrate your *individual rate of return* imagine receiving a $100 loan at 0% interest. How much money could you make with it in one year? It is worth noting that the amount received may also change the amount you can make so consider this too. What you can return, altogether, is your *individual rate of return*

Let us now demonstrate a change in *individual rate of return* by modeling choices by the 25-year-old in our past example who had all their savings stored in their savings account making a paltry 0.07% APY[i]. Their *individual rate of return* is just that, 0.07%. Let us assume that our 25-year-old has $300 to their name and *learns through a catalyst* (more on this later) about an option to put increments of $100 into a 52-week U.S. Treasury

---

[i] I sometimes reluctantly dub the savings account as the "high-yielding checking account" because without a disciplined approach to budgeting and investing, money is often spent in this account anyway.

Bill which makes a 1.00% annualized return. After determining that $100 is an appropriate "safety net" to keep in the bank (wouldn't that be great), our 25-year-old decides that $100 out of the remaining $200 will be used to purchase the Treasury Bill. Their *individual rate of return* then changes from 0.07% to 0.38%.

BEFORE

$$\$300 \; out \; of \; (divided \; by) \; \$300 \; is \; making \; (multiply) \; 0.07\% \; = \; 0.07\%$$

AFTER

$$\begin{aligned} & \$200 \; out \; of \; (divided \; by) \; \$300 \; is \; making \; (multiply) \; 0.07\% \; = \; 0.05\% \\ + \; & \underline{\$100 \; out \; of \; (divided \; by) \; \$300 \; is \; making \; (multiply) \; 1.00\% \; = \; 0.33\%} \\ & \qquad Individual \; Rate \; of \; Return \; = \; 0.38\% \end{aligned}$$

The complexity of measuring your *individual rate of return* can easily increase when you consider that most people have more than one account, more than one loan, and variable rates of return. To be fair, I believe it is impossible to precisely measure opportunity cost, but this step is probably the closest you can come to an accurate figure. Still, try to be as close as you can.

It is worth mentioning that it is not possible to invest yourself in your mathematical best interest. Our parable person cannot put all $300 into 52-week Treasury Bills because they need a "safety net". This is the reason you will hear "live within your means" in fundamental budgeting. Obviously, the lower your standard of living, the lower your "safety net", and the more you can maximize your earnings potential.

Why put in all this work? Your *individual rate of return* is instrumental in evaluating you at your current situation and is a rate we use when communicating performances (as you will see in the coming chapters). When we unravel the information from our *individual rate of return* out, it becomes easier to see that your current interests might not be aligned with your best interest. This is like how the Pareto principle suggests that our interests are not always aligned to our benefit. The Pareto principle, also famously known as the 80/20 rule, states that we often put 20% of our interest in the source that provides 80% of our benefit. Often life moves so fast we need to rebalance ourselves.

In our example, the 25-year-old might need $100 in savings as a mandatory safety net. What if instead of $300 to their name, they started with $290 and it simply was not enough to have another U.S. Treasury Bill investment? Their money would eventually compound over the $300 and would require a rebalancing, a multitude of factors could have changed between first realizing the opportunity and when it became a viable option. For instance, the rate of return on the security could have been below our *individual rate of return*, the mandatory minimum was above our capable contribution, we could have needed a larger “safety net”, and the list goes on. So long as we can maintain a good practice of consistently monitoring our *individual rate of return*, we can keep increasing the value by moving money into a place of our best interest. Here, it would be moving another $100 into a U.S. Treasury Bill when the time came.

Our individual at a net worth of $300, with $100 invested in the U.S. Treasury Bill and $200 in savings, is accruing a *capital allocation, present cost* factor opportunity cost of 0.31% a year (remember $100 must be in reserves). Adapting to a scenario of their best interest will cause an *individual rate of return* of 0.69%.

$$
\begin{aligned}
\$100 \textit{ out of (divided by) } \$300 \textit{ is making (multiply) } 0.07\% &= 0.02\% \\
+ \quad \$200 \textit{ out of (divided by) } \$300 \textit{ is making (multiply) } 1.00\% &= 0.67\% \\
\textit{New Individual Rate of Return} &= 0.69\%
\end{aligned}
$$

Once you finish this book, I encourage you to do your best to theorize, draw out, use a spreadsheet program, etc., to figure out your allocation that nets you the highest *individual rate of return*. Is this value the same as your allocation strategy right now? If not, you may have immediately identified an opportunity cost. Make sure to attribute as many factors as you can, including taxes, fees, and time. Keep note of this and check it over time to see where your values have changed and use it to rebalance if the need arises.

Chapter 5: Future Costs of Capital Allocation

Future costs are expenses we inevitably must spend as a direct result of opportunities or purchases. Analyzing the future costs are critical because they represent the single greatest cause for underestimating the *real costs* of opportunity. Therefore, the *future costs of capital allocation* are the lasting effects of financial decisions.

For instance, when you purchase a car you have simultaneously bought the car insurance, gas, maintenance, registration, depreciation, taxes, upgrades, and all other expenses that you owe in the lifetime of ownership. If you wanted to be as accurate as possible you would find as many of these supplementary *future costs* as possible and amortize them from the date of a purchase. For example, in buying a new car if you found out that the registration every year will be $240, then you can amortize the amount for the following years. You would need to save $20 a month for next year's registration, $10 a month for the following year, then $6.67, and so on for the lifespan of ownership. If you notice, however, some of these values are going to be nearly impossible to quantify even if you possess ungodly self-awareness of your spending patterns. How would you know what your maintenance costs are going to be in the future or how long the ownership of the vehicle will be? This matrix element is the primary reason why we can assume opportunity cost will never be an exact or fixed number.

Even though the sum of *future costs of capital allocation* will not be precisely evaluable it is still valuable. Imagine seeing the difference of a price tag of a car that takes this matrix entry into effect and one that does not. Unfortunately, not seeing the *future costs of capital allocation* reflected in the price does not mean it does not exist and is something we must be mindful of. The cost that this matrix element represents is often more than the purchase price of the opportunity itself!

Chapter 6: Present Costs of Time Allocation

Time is your greatest asset. Consequentially, your time spent and the ability to allocate your time is the most monumental cost factor in opportunity cost. The current time allocation is represented by the *present costs of time allocation* and the most significant reason why the $20 book purchase became more than $300. Pertaining to this factor we must ask ourselves:

- Do our opportunities require an equal amount of time?
- Do our opportunities favor the time value of money?
- Do our opportunities give us flexibility to allocate time?

Trade for Time

In our example, our parable person had to trade 8 hours of time to read the book. If there was a book that presented the same information but was able to do it in 7 hours, obviously the 7-hour version would be more beneficial. The same principle applies for the acquisition of a book. Does one method, such as driving to a bookstore, require you to drive an hour adding to your overall cost?

Time Value of Money

As a rule of thumb, we want our opportunities to give us money as soon as possible and to have to pay debt as far out as possible. For example, we would rather $1,000 today than $1,000 in the future so we can earn interest and we would also rather pay $100,000 over 100 years rather than 1 year. Sometimes there are even incentives to promote this behavior where we need to calculate opportunity cost and the *present costs of time allocation*.

A common technique, particularly among small business, to collect money in accounts receivable (money owed to us) is the 2/10 net 30 discount. There are many variations, but 2/10 net 30 provides the business who owes you money to receive a 2% discount if an amount due is paid within 10 days, or else it is due in full as normal. If the consumer paid on the first of the month you would have 98% of your net amount due (100% - 2% discount for early payment). In a month with 31 days (the best-case scenario in favor of 2/10 net 30) you would need to earn a 2.04% return on the remaining 30 days for you to break even [98% * (1 + 2.04%) = 100%]. At face value 2.04% does not sound like a lot, but when you annualize the figure it is the equivalent of earning a compounded return of 27.85% per year. Not an easy feat, especially not consistently. Yet, this technique is found on almost every accounting software program! Whereas we do want our money sooner and to pay debt later there is a limit to how far we should go.

Sometimes when we try to value opportunity cost of the time value of money, we run into difficulty in quantifying value. One of the reasons that 2/10 net 30 is so popular is that even though it is mathematically hard to conquer, the lenders at higher risk of not paying money owed may be more likely to pay towards a company offering a 2% discount for early payment than one without. It will also be easier to pay less money. That margin of risk might be hard to quantify when deciding to offer the discount. It makes sense, right? How do we figure out the odds of an accounts receivable not being recognized? If we *invert* framing the question from "what are the psychic values" to "the cost is a required minimum 27.85% annualized return, at best, and every month" it becomes easier to logically decide if the decreased risk is worth the venture.

Time Management

Also, in our example the parable person had put themselves in a position to willingly work 8 additional hours of overtime. For most people this is not the case, they cannot simply pick up a shift whenever and earn more money. Additionally, not everyone has the flexibility to change their schedule at a moment's notice. However uncommon this level of time management might be, there are cases where it does exist and should be a goal for us to obtain. Afterall, being able to immediately quickstep into an opportunity that will yield the greatest return is not something you want impeded.

This results in an outstanding difference in calculating opportunity cost and an important lesson on managing our time. However, this does not mean we need to go out and immediately work 3 jobs and 100+ hours a week because it is the mathematical best option. There is something to be said about the power of time to yourself. A balance must be made between the two and that is where the *future costs of time allocation* will enter our evaluation.

Chapter 7: Future Costs of Time Allocation

Because future costs are the greatest cause for underestimating opportunity cost and because time allocation is our most monumental cost factor, that means *future costs of time allocation* is the single greatest element in the opportunity cost matrix. *Future costs of time allocation* are the future commitments to time we owe for pursuing an opportunity and comprise the most significant cost of all, missed opportunities.

Let us go back to the example where the 25-year-old moved the available $200 into the 52-week Treasury Bill. Did we eliminate our opportunity cost completely? From the perspective of the *present cost of capital allocation,* it would appear so, however the *future costs of time allocation* have more to add. In a Treasury Bill you are locked into a specific time commitment (in this case 52-weeks) and forfeit your remaining interest if sold prematurely[i]. What would be the probability that our parable 25-year-old, in the span of 52-weeks, found an opportunity that superseded the yield of the U.S. Treasury Bill? In this case the solution could be as simple as selling the Treasury Bill and investing into the opportunity but what if it were harder to do that? What if the money was not locked into a Treasury Bill but instead in something more illiquid, such as an investment property? We must provide ourselves an exit strategy for all opportunities. We need to ask ourselves vital questions such as:

- What are the costs associated with leaving a venture in case there is a more profitable one?

---

[i] Possibly causing an indirect cost under certain conditions.

- What is the return on a venture that would cause us to change our allocation to a new venture?

We already discussed what the *future costs of capital allocation* mean for buying a car. We automatically sign ourselves up for paying expenses such as registration, right? Well that also means we owe time for driving to the town hall or going online to pay it. We have promised that bit of time. This might be a small example of our *future costs of time allocation* but we would be shocked if we knew exactly how much time is already taken from us by all of the things we do not recognize take time from us. We want to do as much as we can to keep our time to ourselves so that we can continue to put it in our best interest. The concept of buying back your time was very wonderfully demonstrated in *The 4-Hour Work Week* by Time Ferris and is a must read for time management.

The probabilistic nature of *future costs* brings us to another example of how opportunity cost becomes uncertain. How do we measure our probability of finding better alternatives? Additionally, the metric we create to adjust for this becomes wildly different from one person to the next. Some people might have the same bank account all their life while others have a relentless passion and will change from month to month scouring resources for the greatest returns, despite 0.01% differences. We must study our behaviors and simply make the best decisions. There is no need to spend numerous hours on the process, our estimates will do just fine, and because according to the *present costs of time allocation* there is a time-reward factor in studying opportunity cost.

Part 2:

Performance Factors

Chapter 8: Rate of Return

MEASURING PAST PERFORMANCE FACTORS

When we look at past performances, we expect to see what would have happened to our money had we invested with it in the past. In other words, a 1-year, 10% rate of return would make $100 grow to $110. Unfortunately, rates of return are **hardly ever** this rate. The ambiguity for the term "rate of return" results in the greatest cause for miscalculating performance and poses a significant problem for opportunity cost calculations. To make matters worse, language is an art, meaning that the interpretation of the terms may lead to erroneous mathematical results. This means we must know the math ourselves. In an ideal world we would have the day-by-day data but because that is not always practical, we will settle for the next best thing.

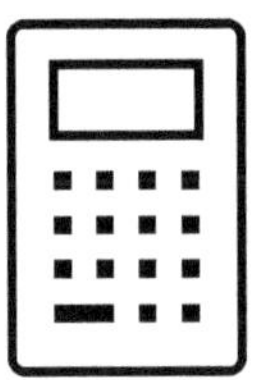

ANNUALIZED MONEY-WEIGHTED ROI

The return you must use is a combination of your **Return on Investment (ROI)** and your **Money-Weighted Rate of Return**.

RETURN ON INVESTMENT (ROI)

The return on investment (ROI) is the actual amount an investment makes after all gains (e.g. dividends, interest, capital gains, disbursements, coupons, etc.) and all expenses (e.g. expense ratios, fees, taxes, cost factors of opportunity cost, etc.). It is pertinent that each factor that goes into an investment, or opportunity, is known and accounted for because they can make a significant difference. Imagine two investors, one who made a 20% return in 364 days and one that made a 19.99% return in 366 days. Without calculating for taxes (assuming they are in a taxable bracket), we might foolishly believe the 20% return was superior. Despite how simple this sounds, not using ROI is surprisingly common.

One misconception of returns, and not using ROI, are the 3-month, 6-month, 1-year, and x-time performances on our favorite stock platforms which only uses price appreciation. That means dividends and other disbursements, that might otherwise be reinvested or collected, are not included. The same goes for taxes and fees (and yes, the commission-free platforms still have regulatory fees). According to these charts, two securities can have the exact same performance when their actual ROI is wildly different because one had a larger dividend. The same is true for when people mistakenly use historical S&P 500 Index data without using the S&P 500 Total Return historical data which accounts for dividends reinvested.

Average rates of return are another example of harmful rates of return. Say we started a new job and are going over the portfolios in the retirement plan. Do we pick the portfolio with the highest percentage and move on with our lives? Unfortunately, to choose the best performer it is not that easy. Just like how statistics can be used to *read* a certain way, rates of return can be similarly framed to *read* differently. Imagine you are an owner of a mutual fund. For three years, your mutual fund grew exactly 10% each year. The *average rate of return* over those three years is 10%.

$$\underline{Year\ 1} \quad \underline{Year\ 2} \quad \underline{Year\ 3}$$

$$Portfolio\ 1: \ \frac{+10\% \quad +10\% \quad +10\%}{3} = 10\%$$

Now imagine you own a mutual find with a performance that is more capricious. Still, over three years this mutual fund's *average rate of return* is also 10%.

$$\underline{Year\ 1} \quad \underline{Year\ 2} \quad \underline{Year\ 3}$$

$$Portfolio\ 2: \ \frac{+10\% \quad -20\% \quad +40\%}{3} = 10\%$$

Are these mutual funds the same despite one being more volatile? Nope. Had you invested $100 in each portfolio, Portfolio 1 would make you $9.90 richer. This is because the first portfolio's actual ROI is 10% and the second portfolio's ROI is only 7.20%. Take an example to the extreme and you will see the difference clearly. A portfolio with $1 invested that goes up 1000% in year one and down 1000% in year two will have an *average rate of return* of 0%, but an ending balance of -$99. Unfortunately, you will see mutual fund companies use this tactic all the time to make their portfolios look better to attract consumers. If you were a shady portfolio manager of portfolio 2 you could compare the two portfolios using the average returns which are equal at 10% because it would make yours look equal, rather than admit to the portfolio being truly inferior.

The difference in types of returns is one of the most misunderstood topics in finance. It is important in opportunity cost because it could make or break your decisions. For most people, the best rate of return, that is often provided, is the **Total Rate of Return**. The total rate of return accounts for all the gains and expenses. The difference, and the reason why the ROI is suggested, is that dividends are reinvested with the total rate of return, which might not be your case. Additionally, you might have added expenses that the total rate of return does not account for. However, the total rate of return is a wonderful place to start.

For demonstration, Acorns is a free app which rounds purchases made to the nearest dollar and automatically invests that difference when the total is $5 or more. You may also do one-time purchases and get rewards for shopping with their partners, making this app a marvelous tool for individuals starting to invest and beginning to budget. Imagine a 25-year old had Acorns and made a one-time contribution of $50 and never used the app again. To find out their ROI they would have to find out the total rate of return for the portfolio they chose to contribute to. If they could not find the total return on the portfolio, they would have to find out how the portfolio is divided and find the total returns of each individual fund. Then they would have to put a weight on the performance based on the portfolio weight. This is like how individual rate of return was calculated in Chapter 4: and shown in Figure 1.

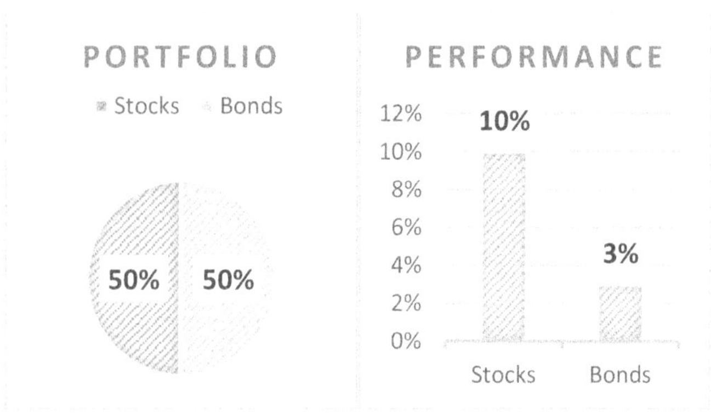

$$50\%\ \textit{of the portfolio made a (multiply)}\ 10\%\ \textit{total return} = 5.00\%$$
$$+\ \ 50\%\ \textit{of the portfolio made a (multiply)}\ 3\%\ \textit{total return} = 1.50\%$$
$$\textit{Individual Rate of Return} = 6.50\%$$

FIGURE 1: ACORNS SIMPLE PERFORMANCE EXAMPLE

However, the total returns do not take into effect Acorn's $1 monthly fee. This leads to a discrepancy between the total return and your ROI. One dollar might not seem like a lot, but after compounding that factor, and all others, it might make or break your decisions!

MONEY-WEIGHTED RATE OF RETURN

A sole $50 investment in Acorns might be relatively easy to find a performance for, however how does it change when contributions are made, especially inconsistent and irregular ones? An investment that went from $1 to $100 with no contributions has a much greater performance than one that went from $1 to $100 with monthly contributions between $1-5. Whereas ROI is the standalone performance, we must also adjust our return based on inflows and outflows. The money-weighted rate of return calculates a percentage that accounts for both the contributions and the withdrawals. However, there is a catch. The formula is complicated and cannot be solved for the percentage unless a code, solver program, or guess and check like method is used. I have provided the daunting equation and an easier to understand excel example below. The sample excel sheet can be found at www.jessierancourt.com/tools

$$Ending\ Balance = Beginning\ Balance * (1 + rate) + \sum_{i=1}^{n} \{Cashflow_i * (1 + rate)^{\left[\frac{total\ periods - period}{total\ periods}\right]}\}$$

Money-Weighted Return Analysis

Goal Seek		Note
Set cell:	$12,000.00	=D375
To value:	$12,000.00	=Ending Balance
By changing cell:	0.23981%	**Effective Rate*
Annualized	**139.71%**	=(1+F6)^A375-1

Period	Day	Contribution/ Withdarawl	Money-Weighted Growth	Formula
0	12/31/2018	$0.00	$10,000.00	=Starting Balance
1	1/1/2019	-$50.00	$9,973.98	=E10*(1+$F$6)+D11
2	1/2/2019	$711.00	$10,708.90	=E10*(1+$F$6)+D12
3	1/3/2019	$685.00	$11,419.58	=E10*(1+$F$6)+D13
4	1/4/2019	-$394.00	$11,052.97	=E10*(1+$F$6)+D14
5	1/5/2019	$70.00	$11,149.47	=E10*(1+$F$6)+D15
6	1/6/2019	$236.00	$11,412.21	=E10*(1+$F$6)+D16
7	1/7/2019	$294.00	$11,733.58	=E10*(1+$F$6)+D17
32	2/1/2019	-$47.00	$11,357.51	=E10*(1+$F$6)+D42
60	3/1/2019	-$460.00	$9,221.59	=E10*(1+$F$6)+D70
152	6/1/2019	$15.00	$6,210.30	=E10*(1+$F$6)+D162
244	9/1/2019	$553.00	$9,148.02	=E10*(1+$F$6)+D254
365	12/31/2019	-$573.00	$12,000.00	=E10*(1+$F$6)+D375
		-$5,724.00		

Figure 2: Money-Weighted Return in Excel Example

In the excel graphic, a random series of data was created to demonstrate an active investment. In the excel sheet, and within the contribution and withdrawal column, you want to include all gains and all expenses that are a direct result of the investment that we discussed with ROI. Once you record all the information, you will want to use Excel's Goal Seek tool to find the periodic rate and thusly, the annualized return. We will cover what the annualized return is, and why we used it in the next chapter on communicating performances.

Periodic Rate

The periodic rate is the rate of return expressed on an interval of time. If you are given the return on 12-months, the periodic rate can express the 1-month equivalent.

Just as there were inefficient ways to adjust for performances, (e.g. simple price appreciation and average rates of return) there are inefficient ways to adjust for your contributions and withdrawals. The thrift savings plan, offered to millions of government employees as a retirement plan, uses a time-weighted return called the "Modified Dietz Method" to calculate portfolio performance. The problem is that the equation attributes a weight to the time contributions or withdrawals are made, which is not exact. The estimation produces a return that when used with historical data does not get you to where you are today. It may be close, but it is inaccurate, and inaccurate performances are going to harm an overall opportunity cost equation.

Chapter 9: Communicating Performances

There is a very specific way to communicate performances correctly. First, we must have a money-weighted return on investment for every one of our opportunities, which takes all factors into consideration, and adjusts for the cashflows. Secondly, we must annualize the returns.

Annualized Rate of Return

An annualized rate of return expresses a rate of return over a given period as the yearly equivalent.

Too often we hear people discussing finance saying the wrong things to communicate their performances. "I made $2,000 investing in XYZ." "The last trade I made gave me a 50% return." Common phrases such as these are useless.

The annualized rate of return is important because it gives us relatability between performances and grants us the ability to weigh the time value of returns. Say, opportunity 1 yielded us a 20% return over 6-months and opportunity 2 yielded us a 30% return over 9-months. At first glance the 30% gain appears to be a better return. However, because the 20% return was made in 2/3 the amount of time, it is more valuable. The equation for annualized rate of return is given by:

$$Annualized\ Rate\ of\ Return = \left(\frac{Amount}{Principal}\right)^{\frac{1}{Time}} - 1$$

Using the annualized rate of return finally allows us to create the individual rate of return described in Chapter 4:.

$$\frac{(\$150\ beginning\ stock\ portfolio)}{out\ of(divided\ by)\$200\ total\ money}\ with\ a\ (multiplied\ by)\ money - weighted\ annaulzied\ ROI\ of\ 10\% = 7.50\%$$

$$+\ \frac{(\$50\ beginning\ bank\ portfolio)}{out\ of(divided\ by)\$200\ total\ money}\ with\ a\ (multiplied\ by)\ money - weighted\ annaulzied\ ROI\ of\ 1\% = 0.25\%$$

$$Annualized, Money - Weighted, Individual\ ROI = 7.75\%$$

The last factor required is the length of time for the performance. A 1-day, 20% annualized return is tremendously different than a 20-year, 20% annualized return because of the proven consistency with the 20-year record. The same is true for using the last 5 years of an opportunity rather than the last 10 because some constant changed. Pretend a business of 10 years added a business partner after 5 years that significantly changed the business for the better. The 10 year looks more reliable by longevity, but the business economics might best be reflected by the 5-year analysis.

This means, past performances are no guarantee of future results. The performance factors we have gone over are for evaluating past performances, although helpful, is not everything.

The main lesson is that it is important to know what rate is being used, how to calculate it, and how to communicate it. This way we can measure our opportunity cost by examining our opportunities, and that of others, appropriately.

Chapter 10: The S&P 500 Index as a Benchmark

Even when provided with a correct performance measurement, a performance still means nothing without an appropriate benchmark.

What is a Benchmark?

A benchmark is a standard which an investment is measured against.

When measuring opportunity cost, we compare the performance of a benchmark against all alternatives to identify the outperforming opportunity. For example, if we were told an opportunity yielded a money-weighted, annualized, ROI of 20% last year, the performance sounds tremendous. However, add to this that the general market gained 30% in the same period, and we discover that 20% was an underperformance.

Therefore, as investors and entrepreneurs seeking opportunity cost, we want to find as many opportunities that we can completely understand and continue to challenge our best alternative against it. The more alternatives gathered, the stronger the ability to grow. Additionally, because conditions of opportunities are subject to change, we must not write any opportunities off for good. This allows us to remain current on the best possible choice.

One such benchmark that must be included in any opportunity cost equation is the Standard & Poor's 500 Index (S&P 500 Index, aka the S&P 500). The S&P 500 Index is one of the best benchmarks, because investments into a low-cost fund that tracks the S&P 500 has proven countless times to outperform most individuals who have attempted to yield superior results.

The capability to passively invest in a high-yielding security provides a wonderful opportunity to satisfy both *capital allocation* and *time allocation*.

***

In one of the most acclaimed investor challenges of all time [11], Warren Buffett, CEO of Berkshire Hathaway and arguably the best investor alive, bet Protege Partners in 2007 to see who could have the best return after ten years. Protege Partners collected their greatest minds to create five "funds-of-funds" to see if they can beat Buffett, the "Oracle of Omaha." Warren Buffett simply chose the S&P 500 index fund (before the 2008 Recession mind you). After 10 years not only did the S&P 500 beat the managed funds, the S&P 500 did so passively. Imagine how many hours the "funds-of-funds" managers spent picking, buying, and selling securities that could have been saved with the set it and forget it S&P 500 index. The S&P 500 index also did not have to adjust for any tax or excessive fees that would usually come with the active investment management.

TABLE 1: WARREN BUFFETT AND PROTEGE PARTNERS FINAL SCORECARD

Source: Berkshire Hathaway 2017 Annual Report

Year	Fund-of-Funds A	Fund-of-Funds B	Fund-of-Funds C	Fund-of-Funds D	Fund-of-Funds E	S&P 500 Index Fund
2008	-16.5%	-7.3%	-21.3%	-29.3%	-30.1%	-37.0%
2009	11.3%	14.5%	21.4%	16.5%	16.8%	26.6%
2010	5.9%	6.8%	13.3%	4.9%	11.9%	15.1%
2011	-6.3%	-1.3%	5.9%	-6.3%	-2.8%	2.1%
2012	3.4%	9.6%	5.7%	6.2%	9.1%	16.0%
2013	10.5%	15.2%	8.8%	14.2%	14.4%	32.3%
2014	4.7%	4.0%	18.9%	0.7%	-2.1%	13.6%
2015	1.6%	2.5%	5.4%	1.4%	-5.0%	1.4%
2016	-3.2%	1.9%	-1.7%	2.5%	4.4%	11.9%
2017	12.2%	10.6%	15.6%	N/A	18.0%	21.8%
Final Gain	**21.7%**	**42.3%**	**87.7%**	**2.8%**	**27.0%**	**125.8%**

The Little Book of Behavioral Investing and *The Little Book of Common Sense Investing* are gems among sources for investment knowledge. In the former cites an annual study called the Dalbar studies, which measures individual investor returns against the S&P 500 index and their attempt to "time the market."

> *"Over the last 20 years, the S&P 500 has generated just over 8% on average each year. Active managers have subtracted 1 to 2 percent from this, so you might be tempted to think that individual investors in equity funds would have earned 6 to 7 percent. However, equity fund investors have managed to reduce this to a paltry 1.9 percent per annum." -James Montier, Author*

The latter book, *The Little Book of Common Sense Investing* by Jack Bogle, examines the 355 equity funds that existed in 1970 and follows their performance against the S&P 500 Index after 36 years to 2006.

- 223 funds no longer exist
- 60 trailed the S&P 500 by 1% or more
- 48 were within an uneventful plus or minus 1%
- 24 overperformed between 1% and 2%; arguably luck
- 6 underperformed when money poured into the funds
- **3/355** truly outperformed the S&P 500 Index

The conclusion Bogle made was that 8/10 of 1% were genuinely able to outperform the S&P500 after 36 years. He suggests that even though the performances of the three were outstanding, what does the reader suspect the next 36 years to look like after seeing how the odds played out.

***

What are some distinguished S&P 500 Index Funds? To name a few, there's Vanguard's VFIAX (also VOO), Fidelity's VXAIX, and Charles Schwab's SWPPX. The difference between the funds are so minimal that sometimes it is not worth the time to compare them.

FINANCIAL ADVISORS

If we accept that the S&P 500 Index fund can outperform most of the industry's fund managers, then why does a percentage of the population pay for a financial advisor? Ideally, it would be because the individual receiving the financial advising would obtain a percentage over the S&P 500 index, including costs, taxes, and fees. If the financial advisor does not provide a benchmark, how would we know that this service is being provided?

This is, of course, unless an advisee does not have the temperament to participate in passive investing (which in fairness is most people), and therefore, the *psychology of opportunity cost* outweighs the *mathematical*. What happens in realty, according to the statistics and as portrayed in the book *Where are the Customer's Yachts?*, is the innocent consumer *pays* for a *poorer performance* than they would have by passively investing in the index fund. If you have a financial advisor and they do not provide this, I highly recommend asking for it or doing the research for yourself.

THE DIFFICULTY

How many investors and entrepreneurs do we know that actively compare themselves to the S&P 500 Index, never mind a benchmark in general? Few to none. Aside from not knowing how to do this, likely reasons could be that it is fundamentally challenging, requires substantial time, and might require tremendous capital. However, there are ways we can simplify the process for the average individual while remaining relatively close to reality.

There are investment apps that provide the ability to do simulated holdings which, although demanding, could work. The criteria would be that the simulated holdings would be put into an S&P500 Total Return Index so that dividends can be included. Additionally, adjustments to the final performance must be made for taxes or any other ancillary effects of an investment had it not been simulated. Furthermore, the simulated holdings would have to address all the inflows and outflows of the alternative. Yet, this method has a few more drawbacks. First, it is a "going forward" approach meaning that it will take some time for results to be known. Secondly, this method takes enormous upkeep and therefore ends up having decreased sustainability (I have yet to see anyone stick to this method).

I have found that the easiest way for the average investor to benchmark against the S&P 500 is to download historical data of the S&P 500 Total Return (^SP500TR) found on Yahoo Finance[i]. Although this does not qualify for an *apples to apples* comparison, the average individual will get very close, at no cost, and with relative simplicity. Beneficially, this method not only allows us to check "going forward" performance but also past performances as well, enabling the ability to make better decisions faster. The hardest part will be creating a "process tree" to account for money-weighting cashflows. Although the math will still overwhelming, having the certainty will be even more rewarding.

---

[i]https://finance.yahoo.com/quote/%5ESP500TR/history?p=%5ESP500TR

Part 3:
Psychological Factors

Chapter 11: Paying Debt or Investing the Difference

The Absolute Value Method

When paying off debt there are two strategies most people are familiar with called the avalanche method and the snowball method. The avalanche method is the act of paying off debts with the highest yield first. This technique *mathematically* pays off **debts** in the most efficient order. The snowball method, popularized by finance icon Dave Ramsey, contrarily suggests that people pay off their debt with the smallest balance first. The action of paying off a debt instills a sense of success with people and although it is not be the most efficient route *mathematically*, it might yield better results than the avalanche method. This is due to psychological factors of opportunity cost which we will discuss soon. However, there is an even more efficient way to *mathematically* increase net worth than both methods.

An example of *present cost, capital allocation* is the very common question of whether to pay debt off or pay only the minimum and invest the difference. *Mathematically*, you will make the most money if you focus your money first into what must be paid and then into the account with the largest rate (making sure they are *apples to apples* remember), regardless of it being debt losing you money or investments making you money. Using the *absolute value method*, you organize your opportunities in order of the rates and work your way largest to smallest.

To help understand the concept, picture all the money you have denominated into one big pile of pennies. You then have buckets set up for each account (debts, banking, investments, etc.) with only the *absolute value* rate painted on them (Figure 3).

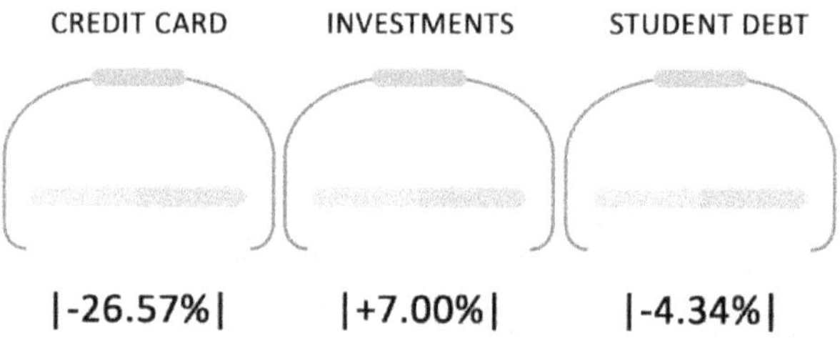

Figure 3: The Absolute Value Method Using Mental Buckets

First, allocate the pennies into the buckets based upon what is required[i], then focus the rest into the highest value bucket. If that bucket fills up, then continue down the line focusing solely on putting each penny in the bucket with the highest yield. Any deviation away from this increases your *present cost of capital allocation* in the opportunity cost equation, *mathematically*. Yet, the absolute value method might still be practically less efficient due to the *psychology of opportunity cost*.

---

[i] Assuming that there is enough money to cover all the minimums or else other factors, such as fees, will apply.

Absolute Value Method				
Details	Credit Card Debt	Investments	Student Debt	Net Worth
Annualized Rate	26.57%	7.00%	4.34%	
Monthly Rate	1.98%	0.57%	0.35%	
Minimum Payment	$25.00	$0.00	$100.00	
1/1/2020	$3,000.00	$0.00	$1,000.00	-$4,000.00
2/1/2020	$2,651.56	$0.00	$903.19	-$3,554.75
3/1/2020	$2,296.20	$0.00	$806.04	-$3,102.24
4/1/2020	$1,933.80	$0.00	$708.54	-$2,642.35
5/1/2020	$1,564.22	$0.00	$610.70	-$2,174.92
6/1/2020	$1,187.31	$0.00	$512.51	-$1,699.82
7/1/2020	$802.92	$0.00	$413.98	-$1,216.89
8/1/2020	$410.91	$0.00	$315.09	-$726.00
9/1/2020	$11.12	$0.00	$215.85	-$226.98
10/1/2020	$0.00	$388.88	$116.26	$272.61
11/1/2020	$0.00	$791.08	$16.32	$774.75
12/1/2020	$0.00	$1,279.23	$0.00	$1,279.23
1/1/2021	$0.00	$1,786.46	$0.00	$1,786.46

Avalanche Method				
Details	Credit Card Debt	Investments	Student Debt	Net Worth
Annualized Rate	26.57%	7.00%	4.34%	
Monthly Rate	1.98%	0.57%	0.35%	
Minimum Payment	$25.00	$0.00	$100.00	
1/1/2020	$3,000.00	$0.00	$1,000.00	-$4,000.00
2/1/2020	$2,651.56	$0.00	$903.19	-$3,554.75
3/1/2020	$2,296.20	$0.00	$806.04	-$3,102.24
4/1/2020	$1,933.80	$0.00	$708.54	-$2,642.35
5/1/2020	$1,564.22	$0.00	$610.70	-$2,174.92
6/1/2020	$1,187.31	$0.00	$512.51	-$1,699.82
7/1/2020	$802.92	$0.00	$413.98	-$1,216.89
8/1/2020	$410.91	$0.00	$315.09	-$726.00
9/1/2020	$11.12	$0.00	$215.85	-$226.98
10/1/2020	$0.00	$272.62	$0.00	$272.62
11/1/2020	$0.00	$774.16	$0.00	$774.16
12/1/2020	$0.00	$1,278.54	$0.00	$1,278.54
1/1/2021	$0.00	$1,785.77	$0.00	$1,785.77

Snowball Method				
Details	Credit Card Debt	Investments	Student Debt	Net Worth
Annualized Rate	26.57%	7.00%	4.34%	
Monthly Rate	1.98%	0.57%	0.35%	
Minimum Payment	$25.00	$0.00	$100.00	
1/1/2020	$3,000.00	$0.00	$1,000.00	-$4,000.00
2/1/2020	$3,033.99	$0.00	$526.86	-$3,560.85
3/1/2020	$3,068.66	$0.00	$52.05	-$3,120.71
4/1/2020	$2,672.68	$0.00	$0.00	-$2,672.68
5/1/2020	$2,215.76	$0.00	$0.00	-$2,215.76
6/1/2020	$1,749.78	$0.00	$0.00	-$1,749.78
7/1/2020	$1,274.57	$0.00	$0.00	-$1,274.57
8/1/2020	$789.92	$0.00	$0.00	-$789.92
9/1/2020	$295.67	$0.00	$0.00	-$295.67
10/1/2020	$0.00	$204.33	$0.00	$204.33
11/1/2020	$0.00	$705.48	$0.00	$705.48
12/1/2020	$0.00	$1,209.47	$0.00	$1,209.47
1/1/2021	$0.00	$1,716.31	$0.00	$1,716.31

Chapter 12: When the Right Answer is Not the Right Answer

Without trying to steal a page from Howard Mark's book, *The Most Important Thing*, the *psychology of opportunity cost* is the most important section of this book. Because even if you know the *mathematics* behind evaluating opportunity costs, the final execution is everything. In the chapter on Paying Debt or Investing the Difference, we discussed how *mathematically* you will decrease your opportunity cost if you home in on the highest *absolute valued* rate, whether debt or investment. However, according to studies of debt and investing, it is easier said than done.

The reason why Dave Ramsey has built his whole pedagogy around the mathematically inferior *snowball method* is not because he believes it is mathematically superior. Instead, he understands that in practice the satisfaction received by paying off debt leaves people feeling vindicated by the results of their work and hungry for more results. This far surpasses the effort of trying to do the right thing and failing because the methods lack sustainability. This is when the right answer, in terms of what is most mathematically efficient, is not the right answer, because the execution did not exist.

One such example is a gentleman who told me he visited a financial advisor whose advice it was to, instead of paying more towards his low-interest mortgage, he should pay the minimum and invest the difference. A *rational, mathematical* decision, yes. The sad truth was that the gentleman changed the process, even though automated, with market cycles. Additionally, he was not in control of his spending causing him to "dip into" the funds. Over time, the fund contributions diminished.

Ultimately, he would have been better off accepting a lower return by paying his house off sooner!

Another infamous and paradoxical behavior pattern to opportunity cost is in handling credit card debt. Some mathematical techniques around solving credit card debt is using a balance transfer offer and lower-interest debt. There are credit cards with a promotion to transfer debt from one credit card to another and not pay interest for a year or more for a 3-5% fee. Ideally, this method involves:

1. Transferring the balance to a credit card with 0% interest for a year or more and pay a fee
2. Pay only the minimum to the credit card and instead invest the money in the best opportunity
3. Seek new opportunities for higher growth
4. When your 0% interest period is finished, sweep everything from the opportunity to the credit card or repeat as needed

However, without changing credit card behaviors we end up worse off than where we began. Due to psychological tendencies, what usually happens is:

1. Transfer the balance to a credit card with 0% interest for a year or more and pay a fee
2. Maybe invest for a while but do not stick with it
3. Use credit cards with the mentality it is all 0% or that we can forever transfer balances for 0%
4. End up with more debt and little to nothing saved

Again, using lower-interest debt to pay credit cards off has the same effect. This can include using a loan against a retirement plan or a home to pay off credit card debt. Typically, the rates on these loans will be significantly less than what a credit card issues. However, without fixing the source of the problem, handling credit cards, this frequently results in a new loan and *more* credit card debt.

With investing, sometimes great performances can lead to some very poor performances. As an example, we covered how a low-cost S&P 500 Index Fund, over time, generally outperforms investors. Imagine a day trader who was successful once, or even a couple of times for that matter, and thusly continued to practice this investing style, despite the statistics showing this to be almost certainly folly. Combine this with an inability to benchmark against the S&P 500 and problems snowball.

However, and this is the beauty of the *psychology of opportunity cost*, sometimes this person's day trading could lead to better performances than passive investing simply because the trader is more interested in managing their finances and creates a better habit. Meaning, even if they only get a lackluster 5% return day trading it would be better than a bad habit 3% from passive investing.

To evaluate your ability to handle the *psychology of opportunity cost,* you must use your past results, really understand yourself and your behaviors, ask the people who might tell you truthfully, and comprehend that we have inborn *psychological biases* we cannot avoid.

Chapter 13: Cognitive Biases

When evaluating opportunity cost, we must take measures to protect against our biases. Biases are the innate tendencies we have as humans to think and behave irrationally. These biases obstruct our rational, opportunity cost decision making to such a degree that even by recognizing them, we cannot entirely rid ourselves of them. We can, however, lower our fair statistical share of human misjudgment by being aware of these biases and factoring them into our evaluation processes. Therefore, we must collect an understanding of as many biases as we can and continue to remind ourselves of the significance behind each one.

For instance, the social desirability bias indicates that humans have a pattern of responding in a way that is perceived as more socially appropriate rather than the ones reflective of one's true thoughts. We can apply this bias to opportunity cost and how it pertains to communicating performances as an example.

We often do not disclose our poor performances with others partly due to not knowing how to communicate performances and in part due to the social desirability bias. When learning about opportunities we want to know all the aspects, so why is it that when we tell others we skim over unflattering details even if the overall performance is respectable? The answer: a desire for social status. When either person communicating about performances fails to disclose the details of the whole, it puts both at a loss. One person will not get the full details of an opportunity and the other will reinforce overestimating their actual performance.

Once we recognize a pattern of a bias, we want to give ourselves the tools for mitigating them. In this instance saying "I don't know at this moment" or "I'll get back to you" is a perfectly reasonable answer for your performance instead of communicating fragments. We have seen how complicated evaluating performance can be so not having it on hand every moment is expected. Additionally, we want to harness the humility and integrity that comes from having and communicating poor performances. We all get them; it is perfectly natural. The faster we can be honest and upfront about them the sooner we can realize where better opportunities exist. Lastly, if we surround ourselves with people in an environment that is understanding of the swings of opportunity there will be less pressure to succumb to social desirability.

As much as we will want to rid ourselves completely of these silly errors, we cannot. Even the largest companies are not free of them. For instance, the development of the Amazon Web Service (AWS) is an exemplary tale of the overconfidence bias which is a tendency of overestimating our skills and competencies.

In an interview with David Rubenstein, Jeff Bezos claims that unlike other product launches (Amazon.com,

Kindle, and Echo), which received competition after a typical two years, the AWS project "faced no like-minded competition for **seven years** [9]." Bezos then claims that although it was an incredible confluence of reasons, it was most likely because the established software companies overlooked Amazon as a software enterprise. These already established software companies had an *overconfidence bias* because they were the top performers in their industry and led them to ignore the potential in a sector which Amazon now controls roughly 33% of the $100 billion cloud-based markets, almost double that of the runner up [10].

To cover all the biases of opportunity cost would take a whole other fascinating (and frankly much needed) book[i]. Therefore, take from this chapter the application of biases in opportunity cost so you can continue to apply them.

---

[i] This speech by Charlie Munger is a must watch for biases https://www.youtube.com/watch?v=pqzcCfUglws&t=3163s

Part 4:
Opportunity Factors

Chapter 14: The Opportunities You Already Have

On the forefront of opportunity cost decision making is Charlie Munger, Vice Chairman of Berkshire Hathaway. During the 2006 Berkshire Hathaway Annual Meeting, Munger had this to say about opportunity cost:

> *"In the real world, you have to find something that you can understand that's the best you have available. And once you've found the best thing, then you measure everything against that because it's your opportunity cost... And the right way to think about investing is to act thinking about your best opportunity cost [11]." -Charlie Munger, Vice Chairman of Berkshire Hathaway*

Munger claims that to think about opportunity cost correctly, we must find the thing we understand and is the best opportunity available. As we go through life, we naturally identify the opportunity we believe is our best available opportunity. Due to the diversity of human experiences, this best opportunity becomes a specialized expertise in our "circle of competence."

Circle of Competence

A term used to express your range of familiarity within subject areas.

Therefore, this proficiency gives us a distinct, strategic advantage over individuals outside our same "circle of competence". Conversely, this means we have a noticeable disadvantage outside of our circle.

If an individual grew up on an airport and worked their entire life as an aircraft mechanic, they will undoubtedly develop a high-level of ability in the aviation industry. They might be able to recognize problems and theorize solutions which someone outside the industry would never think of. The same thing goes for the companies that the mechanic has seen grow consistently or have potential for growth.

This is not to say that we cannot venture outside our areas of familiarity, but that it takes more time and commitment. Instead, you might want to find another individual whose "circle of competence" compliments or completes yours. This way you can stay within your area and multiply your understanding by your network. As the saying goes, "Your network is your net worth."

Chapter 15: People are the Catalyst for Change

Think back to the last time you discovered a new opportunity or became comfortable enough to finally act on one. One of the most important questions to ask ourselves is, "What was the impetus for the change?"

The answer for finding new opportunities is plain and simple, it is people. Previously, we discussed how you have a unique advantage that no one else does because you are the only copy of you on this Earth. This means there are billions of others with different competitive advantages for you to learn from. As Bill Nye once said,

"Everyone you will ever meet knows something that you don't" and it is 100% true.

The best part is that you do not need to know someone on a personal level for you to surround yourself with their thoughts and concepts. You can have the articulated wisdom of Janet Yellen and Abigail Johnson just by reading. This also does not limit you to alive people either; we have generations of great thinkers to learn from.

SURROUND YOURSELF WITH THE RIGHT ENVIRONMENT

Given that people are the key to success, we want to make sure we surround ourselves with a passion driven environment. Sometimes I hear people say that they do not have this kind of environment available. In response, I like to quote Tony Robins, who once said, "It's not the lack of resources, it's your lack of resourcefulness." If you do not think you have a goal structured community, then create one. Passion attracts passion.

Chapter 16: The Speed of Opportunity Cost

Finding rewarding opportunities is a great thing but finding them faster is even better. Opportunities rarely come out of nowhere and present themselves to you. Therefore, we must always be active in our search for better opportunities. You have probably heard the phrase, “the time value of money” and opportunities are no different. As a quick example, someone who is 25 years old and put $6,000 a year into a Roth IRA will, with a 7% annualized return, net a balance of $1,287,657.42 in 40 years versus $1,197,810.67 if it were done one year later and only had 39 years to grow. That is a gigantic

$89,846.75 difference that $6,000 can make for learning something only one year prior.

$$FV = \$6{,}000\ Contributions * \sum_{n=0}^{40} (1 + 7\%\ \mathrm{Return})^{n} = \$1{,}287{,}657.42$$

$$FV = \$6{,}000\ Contributions * \sum_{n=0}^{39} (1 + 7\%\ \mathrm{Return})^{n} = \$1{,}197{,}810.67$$

Presenting opportunities like a factor of time value is important because opportunities often cascade into other opportunities as well. In our example of the Roth IRA, it is likely that a conversation about Roth IRAs can breed conversations about a Roth 401(k). It is likely that tax-advantaged retirement plans can bring to light tax-advantaged health care plans and so on.

Chapter 17: The Velocity of Opportunity Cost

The moment you find out about an opportunity an imaginary timer should start going off in your head. The time spent idling is a massive component to evaluating opportunity cost. This goes especially for the individuals who are trying to "time the market" with their investments. It is rarely the percentage gain that leads to bad investor performances, but rather the percentages that could have been made elsewhere. If you receive a paycheck and you consider that after all bills, expenses, and miscellaneous you can allocate $1,000, then the time starts ticking. You need to find the best possible place for that $1,000 as soon as you can. If you know that you can put it into an opportunity and choose not to, hesitate due to uncertainty, or whatever, then your *velocity of opportunity cost* is increasing your cost.

This does not mean you have to buy into an opportunity or spend your money in that very moment. If your impression is that sitting on the money is the best thing to do, then that is a perfectly fine exercise of allocation, so long as it turns out correct. However, you will never know until time shows you the opportunity cost. Sadly, if you never measure your opportunity cost, you might never find out.

Chapter 18: The Acceleration of Opportunity Cost

Having huge success in evaluating and acting on opportunities comes with a toll, a slowing rate of change. Opportunities not only become sparser, but the changes in percentage points precipitously decline as a person advances their erudition. The person who has only a bank account at 0.03% APY has many more options available to increase their wealth and can see much more dramatic effects of their efforts than an owner of a well-establish Fortune 500 company. For instance, the person yielding 0.03% APY in a bank account can increase their *personal rate of return* by 3,333% by investing the money instead into a 52-week U.S. Treasury Bill yielding 1.00% annualized. However, if you are the business prodigy behind the next Apple making exponential returns year after year, it becomes challenging to find better opportunities.

$$\frac{Treasury\ Bill\ at\ 1.00\%}{Bank\ Account\ at\ 0.03\%} = 3{,}333\%\ Increase$$

$$\frac{Stocks\ at\ 7.00\%}{Treasury\ Bill\ at\ 1.00\%} = 700\%\ Increase$$

In closing, do not be discouraged if you start to observe *the velocity of opportunities* or *the speed of opportunities* decrease as you continue your erudition. This is not a sign of weakness but of strength. Finally, just because these metrics decrease does not mean your passion must either. Enjoy the journey and the pieces will fall into place.

Opportunities

Opportunities for readers to continue their financial literacy

BOOKS

- *A Random Walk Down Wallstreet by Burton G. Malkiel*
  - Best for beginner investors
- *Buffettology by Mary Buffett et al.*
  - Investing techniques
- *The 4-Hour Work Week by Tim Ferris*
  - Time management
- *Get What's Yours by Laurence J. Kotilkof et al.*
  - Maximizing Social Security
- *Your Score by Anthony Davenport et al.*
  - Understanding credit scores
- *Poor Charlie's Almanack by Charlie Munger*
  - The behavioral psychology of finance
- *Rich Dad Poor Dad by Robert T.* Kiyosaki
  - Personal finance fundamentals
- *The Compound Effect by Darren Hardy*
  - The snowball effect of habits
- *Think and Grow Rich by Napoleon Hill*
  - Motivational and inspiring

YOUTUBE

- The Oracle's Classroom
  - Fundamental Financial Analysis
- Graham Stephen
  - Real Estate, Credit Cards, Personal Finance

- Mark J. Kohler
  - Tax and Legal advice
- Book Launchers
  - Creating and publishing a book
- Self-Publishing with Dale
  - Creating and publishing a book

MISC

- Meetup.com
  - Find like-minded people in your community
- Doctorofcredit.com
  - Finding the great savings accounts and credit cards
- Treasurydirect.gov
  - Purchasing government securities
- Vanguard.com
  - Investing in low-cost index funds and securities
- Fiverr.com
  - Access to freelancer network
- Intuit Mint
  - Budgeting
- Quicken
  - Business financial planning and budgeting
- KDP.com
  - Create and distribute paperback and kindle books
- Acx.com
  - Create and distribute audiobooks
- Jessierancourt.com
  - Stay up to date on the author's work

Acknowledgments

Thank you for taking the time to read into an aspect of personal finance that needs to be elaborated on. While we most certainly can dive into some of the chapters with more breadth, you should have enough information now to help navigate your way through your financial allocations with more clarity. In writing this book, I realized just how much more we need to know about opportunity cost and how much potential there is to break into a market. I hope the readers not only find this book fascinating, but it pushes them to engage in another study, furthering their passion.

References

[1] O. U. Press, "Opportunity Cost," [Online]. Available: https://www.oxfordreference.com/view/10.1093/oi/authority.20110810105528518.

[2] "National Average Wage Index," 2018. [Online]. Available: https://www.ssa.gov/oact/cola/AWI.html.

[3] F. D. I. Corporation, "Weekly National Rates and Rate Caps - Weekly Update," [Online]. Available: https://www.fdic.gov/regulations/resources/rates/.

[4] W. Bank, "Inflation," Federal Reserve Bank of St. Louis, [Online]. Available: https://fred.stlouisfed.org/series/FPCPITOTLZGUSA.

[5] M. D. K. K. D. C. J. Zorn, "The impact of hiring directors' choice-supportive bias and escalation of commitment on CEO compensation and dismissal following poor performance: A multimethod study," *Strat. Mgmt. J.,* vol. 41, pp. 308-339, 2020.

[6] *Concorde : A Supersonic Story.* [Film]. BBC, 2017.

[7] *Why Planes Don't Fly Faster.* [Film]. Wendover Productions, 2017.

[8] O. Svenson, "ARE WE ALL LESS RISKY AND MORE SKILLFUL THAN OUR FELLOW DRIVERS," 1981. [Online]. Available: https://www.semanticscholar.org/paper/ARE-WE-ALL-LESS-RISKY-AND-MORE-SKILLFUL-THAN-OUR-Svenson/ad37e00352406dd776bc010769489b2412951c7d.

[9] J. Bezos, Interviewee, *Amazon CEO Jeff Bezos on The David Rubenstein Show.* [Interview]. 19 September 2018.

[10] F. Richter, "Amazon LEads $100 Billion Cloud Market," Statista, 11 February 2020. [Online]. Available: https://www.statista.com/chart/18819/worldwide-market-share-of-leading-cloud-infrastructure-service-providers/.

[11] B. Hathaway, "2017 Annual Report," 2018. [Online]. Available: https://www.berkshirehathaway.com/letters/2017ltr.pdf.

[12] "Warren Buffett Archive, 2006 Annual Meeting," CNBC, 2006. [Online]. Available: https://buffett.cnbc.com/2006-berkshire-hathaway-annual-meeting/.

[13] R. Lane, "Warren Buffett: My Greatest Investing Advice And The Investments Everyone Should Make," 28 September 2017. [Online]. Available:

https://www.forbes.com/sites/randalllane/2017/09/20/warren-buffett-my-greatest-investing-advice-and-the-investments-everyone-should-make/#2e132255593e.

[14] "STRATEGIES FOR EFFECTIVE FACEBOOK WALL POSTS: A STATISTICAL REVIEW," Buddy Media, 2011.

[15] O. Svenson, "ARE WE ALL LESS RISKY AND MORE SKILLFUL THAN OUR FELLOW DRIVERS," 1981. [Online]. Available: https://www.semanticscholar.org/paper/ARE-WE-ALL-LESS-RISKY-AND-MORE-SKILLFUL-THAN-OUR-Svenson/ad37e00352406dd776bc010769489b2412951c7d.

[16] R. Lane, "Warren Buffett: My Greatest Investing Advice And The Investments Everyone Should Make," 28 September 2017. [Online]. Available: https://www.forbes.com/sites/randalllane/2017/09/20/warren-buffett-my-greatest-investing-advice-and-the-investments-everyone-should-make/#2e132255593e.

Index

www.ingramcontent.com/pod-product-compliance
Ingram Content Group UK Ltd.
Pitfield, Milton Keynes, MK11 3LW, UK
UKHW021933190726
13853UKWH00004B/1420